Larry L. McSwain
Kay Wilson Shurden

Call Waiting
God's Invitation to YOUTH

JUDSON PRESS
PUBLISHERS SINCE 1824

VALLEY FORGE

Call Waiting: God's Invitation to Youth

Larry L. McSwain and Kay Wilson Shurden
Consulting Editor: Cassandra D. Williams
© 2005 by Judson Press, Valley Forge, PA 19482-0851
All rights reserved.

Library of Congress Cataloging-in-Publication Data

McSwain, Larry L.
    Call waiting : God's call to youth / Larry L. McSwain and Kay Wilson Shurden.
        p. cm.
    Includes bibliographical references.
    ISBN 0-8170-1481-0 (alk. paper)
    1. Christian youth—Religious life. 2. Vocation—Christianity. I. Shurden, Kay Wilson. II. Title.
    BV4531.3.M42 2005
    248.8'3—dc22   2005019376

09 08 07 06 05   5 4 3 2 1

To our grandchildren
Emily, Audrey, Ben, Sam, and Langley
of the Shurden lineage
and
Hannah, Dillon, Joshua, and Luke
of the McSwain clan
and to
Shurden and McSwain offspring
yet to be born
with
the prayer
that our stories
may help you find
God's calling for your lives

Contents

Acknowledgments

WE, KAY AND LARRY, ARE GRATEFUL TO MANY who have helped us in this venture.

First, without the encouragement and support of Margaret Dee Bratcher and John Dunaway, leaders of Mercer Commons of Mercer University, this project never would have been completed. Their enthusiastic support for what we set out to do, along with funding from the university grant from the Lilly Endowment, Inc., made this book possible. Thank you, Dee and John. And thank you, Lilly Endowment.

Our spouses, Walter B. Shurden and Rebecca Sue McSwain, have been a constant encouragement to us. They have read the manuscript and offered their reactions and suggestions for improving it. More important are their abiding love and support for us.

A number of youth ministers read the manuscript from the perspective of youth. Rev. Brett Foster, youth pastor of Hendricks Avenue Baptist Church, Jacksonville, Florida, gave useful insights from the perspective of one who works extensively with today's youth. McAfee School of Theology students also assisted by reviewing our work, and so we are grateful to Jody Long, Jenny Sommers, Andrew Jones, and Matt Duvall for their perceptions of language and concepts that communicate. Students in the undergraduate capstone class on vocation at Mercer University, taught by William Loyd Allen during the spring of 2004, read the manuscript. Cassandra Williams, managing editor of Judson Press, has invested talent, creativity, and her own insights in major editing of our original work. She has developed the "Appendix for Leaders," for which we are grateful. We thank each one but take full responsibility for what has been written.

Finally, we are grateful to each other. The two of us have been friends for many years, but this is our first venture in working together. Our callings have been strengthened by this sharing of ideas.

Welcome from the Authors

THE WORLD CAN BE PRETTY CONFUSING AT times. By the time we reach adolescence, we have received literally thousands of messages about who we are supposed to be and what we should do with our lives. Different voices pull us in all sorts of directions and present us with countless choices. How do we find clear direction toward the paths that are right for us? This book is designed to help you answer this question for yourself. It was written especially for people ages sixteen to twenty, because that's when you make decisions that affect how you will spend your adult life.

When Christians talk about the path that God would have each of us take in life, they use the word *call*. *Call* is one of those churchy words that rarely gets defined—as if everyone should know what it means—but seems to mean a whole lot of different things. Sometimes call is spoken of in serious tones as if it's a lofty honor reserved for a few: "He received *the call*." Sometimes it seems like a terrible burden: "I am so tired of kids, but I'm stuck because teaching is *my calling*!" And far too often people use the word *call* carelessly, suggesting things such as it's part of their calling to have a fancy car.

The truth is that religious people have been struggling for centuries to understand exactly what call is, so if you're confused about yours, you are in good company. Call is hard to define. Of the many, many voices we hear in our lives, some can help us discover our call, but no single human voice can answer the question, "What is the call for my life?" So rather than provide a formula for pinpointing your call, this book explores call, identifying its key characteristics. It also offers guidance for figuring out what call looks like in your own life.

The issue of call is essential for anyone who chooses to live as a follower of Jesus. We have spent our lives seeking to understand and practice our own callings and helping others do the same. Although we still have a lot to learn, we want to share with you what we have learned so far. We hope we can help you avoid some mistakes and some unnecessary detours in the years ahead, but even more, we hope we can encourage you to dream big, to trust yourself, and to trust that God is with you on your life journey.

In the following pages, in addition to learning key points about Christian calling, you will find stories from the Bible, stories of other young people, and stories from our lives. Our hope is that you will find connections between these stories and your own story. The goal is for you to explore God's calling for you, so each chapter ends with a reflection section and journal space to help you listen for the voice of God and to the voice of your true self. We would like you to commit yourself to participating in the reflection activities. They are designed to make this whole "call thing" real for you.

We want to be sure, though, that you respond in ways that are true to you. You may want to get an additional journal or a sketchbook so you can sometimes draw instead of write. If you are one of those people who likes to "process" things mentally, you may want to set aside enough time to take a walk. Or you may want to invite a friend to be a calling companion so you can discuss the reflection exercises. Finally, make sure you have a favorite Bible on hand in case you want to further explore the biblical stories of call.

Before you get started, though, why don't we take a moment for introductions:

MY NAME IS KAY. I retired four years ago after twenty-five years of working as a family therapist, helping families go through tough times, such as divorce, the death of a loved one, or substance abuse. That's quite unlike what I set out to do four decades ago. I expected to become a missionary to Africa, so after graduating from high school, I went off to college to study religion. Growing up in First Methodist Church, Greenville, Mississippi, I had heard exciting tales of missionaries and had also learned that overseas mission work was one of the few ministry choices open to women, so I opted to go into missions.

During college my path took a turn. I married a man who was planning to be a minister and switched majors to elementary education so I could support us through the seminary years. The change worked out great because I loved teaching young children. Over the years, I completed master's and doctoral degrees and worked as a college professor. My path turned toward family therapy through a course I took as part of my doctoral program. It dealt with the development of women in American society, and through it I began to see that women did not have to be limited to roles of the past. I began to ask myself two questions: "What excites me most?" and "What needs to be done in the world?" My answers brought me to the field of family therapy, where I could help people make their families places where all members are encouraged to be what God has gifted them to be—in relationships, in work, and in church. The dream of inviting others to be their true selves is one of the reasons I worked with Larry McSwain on this book.

I'M LARRY. Considering my background, I am amazed by the opportunities I have had to serve God. Until I finished eighth grade, I lived in Pond Creek, Oklahoma, a small community where my father was a Chevrolet dealer. Since his business was across the street from my school, I worked there some afternoons doing odd jobs. I also worked on a farm my father bought. One of my favorite memories is of my dad letting me drive our pickup for the first time.

After I finished the eighth grade, we moved to a small cattle ranch about a hundred miles away, so I had to adjust to living in a new community, attending a smaller school, and going to church in a town twelve miles from home. Most of my summers were spent working on the ranch, which meant long days with time to wonder about my life. By the time I was a sophomore in high school, I was actively talking to God about what I should do. I had become a Christian at the age of nine, and my childhood pastor had encouraged me to go into the pastoral ministry. I was interested in a lot of things, though, and I thought about staying on the farm, becoming an architect, or going into dentistry. Soon I found myself impatiently praying to God, "Lord, I would like to do with my life what you want, but I need to know more about what that is."

I had attended a youth assembly called Falls Creek a couple of times and appreciated their Bible studies, recreation, and spiritually charged worship services, so during the summer of my junior year, I prayed that I would find an answer during my week at Falls Creek. During that time, the sense that God was calling me to a full-time Christian vocation unfolded, and by the end of the week, I knew that God wanted me to give my life to sharing the gospel as a minister who works full-time in the church. I publicly declared that intention, and when I returned home, I shared the news with my family and church. I have spent more than forty years trying to live out the call I felt that night as an ordained minister and teacher of pastors.

Now that we've told a bit of our stories, why don't you take a few minutes to think about your own story.

For Reflection

1. How would you respond if you had to briefly answer the question, "Who are you?"

2. What experiences stand out in your life?

3. Are you able to talk about your life with God?

4. What dreams do you have for the future?

5. How has God influenced those dreams?

An Invitation

SO YOU'RE WATCHING YOUR FAVORITE MUSIC videos and you're thinking, *Hey, I could do that! I* should *do that…lotsa money, lotsa fun!* Is that call? Not even close.

Or you're searching the Web and you get a pop-up about the next *American Idol* audition. Is this a sign? Should you go for it? Is this call? *Annnnt!* (Buzzer sound.) Wrong again!

Or you ride in a bike-a-thon to raise money for a children's hospital and you begin to feel guilty. You say, "I *must* become a doctor so I can help sick children." But you barely passed biology and you don't even like to *go* to the doctor. Are you ignoring your call? Nope.

Or your grandfather gives his annual "This kid's gonna be the next…(fill in the blank here)!" speech at your birthday party. You smile back at your beaming family, but there's a sick feeling in your stomach. If you let them down, have you rejected God's call? Uh, probably not.

Have you seen the movie *Sister Act*? If you haven't, here's the 411. Vegas lounge singer Delores, played by Whoopi Goldberg, is sent to a convent to hide from the mobster boyfriend who wants to kill her. Delores, or "Sister Mary Clarence," as she's known in the convent, takes over the choir, and it goes from boring a few church members to drawing huge crowds and media attention. Along the way, Delores makes some discoveries about herself, her talents, and her calling in life. But she's not the only one. One night novice Sister Mary Robert brings "Mary Clarence" an alarm clock to help her get up in time for morning prayers. They begin to chat, and Delores asks Mary Robert if she always knew she wanted to be a nun. Mary Robert replies, "I've always known I had a call to a life of service to God, but I've always felt that there was something inside me that I want to give; something that's only me and nobody else."

❀ Call is something that all Christians share but that each of us has in a special way.

We all share the *same call* to a life of service, and we each have a *unique calling* that uses the extraordinary person each of us is. So let's take a look at how one person first got word of his unique calling.

The Call of Moses (Exodus 3:1-12)

You know this story. The baby Moses was placed in a basket by his mom and put into the Nile River to keep him safe from the Egyptians. Pharaoh's daughter found him and raised him as her own son. We can imagine that he had all the perks of royalty growing up, but things really changed later. One day when he was about twenty, Moses saw an Egyptian beating a slave, and to rescue the slave, he killed the Egyptian. This was an offense punishable by death, so Moses ran away across the Nile and far into the desert country of Midian. He eventually became a shepherd for a man named Jethro and married Jethro's daughter. One day many years later, Moses saw a strange site as his flock was grazing in the hill country. A ways off he saw a bush that was on fire but didn't burn up, and when he went to check it out, God spoke to him from the bush.

"Moses! Moses!"

"I'm right here!" Moses replied, approaching the bush.

"Don't come any closer. Take off your sandals—this is holy ground. I am the God who was worshiped by your ancestors, Abraham, Isaac, and Jacob." Then God went on to explain the purpose of the meeting: "I have indeed seen the suffering of my people in Egypt. I have heard their cries for help and seen how cruel the Egyptians are to them. I am going to take them out of Egypt and bring them to a wonderful place, so I need you to go lead them for me."

Moses' first response was "No way! Who am I to do such a thing?" but God assured him by promising, "I will be with you." So Moses headed back to Egypt for what turned out to be the biggest job of his life.

❧ Call is an invitation.

Notice that when God told Moses what needed to be done and Moses said, "Not me!" God didn't respond with "Hey, I'm God, so you *will* do it." Nor did God threaten, "If you don't, you'll be sorry." Nor did God promise, "If you do this, I'll give you a fun life." God simply said, "This is what needs to be done. You are the right person for the job, and *I will be with you.*" For Moses, the way God dealt with him would have been startling. Historical study reveals that in Midian and in Egypt, people worshiped many gods and believed in magic. They believed the gods would punish or reward them according to what they did. They also believed that they could summon a god's presence by speaking his or her secret name. As the story continues, Moses asks for God's name so he can give it to the

Hebrew slaves in Egypt. God advises Moses to tell the people that "I Am" or, perhaps even a better translation, "I will be with you" sent him. No coercion. No manipulation. No threats. No magic. God *invites* Moses to a task and promises to be with him as he carries it out. That's the way call works. It's an invitation that reads like this:

You're Invited!

WHAT: To Partnership
WHERE: In the Church and the World
WHEN: Now and Forever
Love,
God

RSVP: Please respond with all of your life.
P.S. I will be with you no matter what happens.

We'll look at each part of this invitation in the next chapters of *Call Waiting*, but before you read on, do some journaling or connect with your discussion partner and explore the questions below.

For Reflection

❖ Call is something that all Christians share but that each of us has in a special way.
❖ Call is an invitation.

1. What are some ways people respond to invitations?
2. Is the idea of call as an invitation new to you? Does it excite you? Frighten you? Confuse you?

3. What are the voices that you hear when you think about the choices that you will be making over the next few years? How do you decide which voice to listen to? Whose voice is strongest?

4. When you think about the story of Moses, do you connect with Moses? Or does his story seem too different from your life?

5. Think about how different our faith would be had Moses said, "No thanks, God!" What are the results when people say no to God's invitation?

6. God told Moses that the ground where they met was holy. Where is your holy ground—that is, where do you feel close to God? How did you find it?

7. Read the stories below and think about questions you might ask or suggestions you would make to each person if you could speak to him or her personally.

S., a freshman in high school, has been involved in her church most of her life. Her parents took her to Sunday school as a baby, and she still attends nearly every Sunday. She is active in her youth group and worked in vacation Bible school last summer. She is popular, likes to be around people, and tends to be the center of attention whenever her friends get together. She's good at art and music and does well in school. She's fortunate to know she'll have the opportunity to go to college, but at this point, she doesn't have a clue what to study, except that she says she wants to live her life in a way that gives her lots of happiness. In a recent discussion about how Christians know the will of God, she said, "My parents tell me it's an inner feeling of doing what feels right to you."

R., a sophomore at a nearby state university, spent the summer as an intern with the minister of youth at his church. Talking with his pastor, he asks, "How do I know if God is calling me to the ministry? Two years ago I became a

Christian after a friend at school spoke to me about how Jesus died for me. I didn't grow up in the church, so this was new to me. Since that time, I have found a new meaning in my life. I wake up every morning wanting to know more about God. I read the Bible to understand it all better. Somehow I have this feeling God wants me to become a minister and spend my life sharing God's love with other people. But how can I know this is really what God wants?"

M., a junior in high school, is very busy. She is involved in youth group, earns good grades in school, plays clarinet in the school band, and is a cheerleader. She frequently visits Internet chat rooms for young people to discuss her faith. Recently she did a search on vocation and found many Web sites on the topic. She started talking with her chat room contacts about how God calls us. Some of the girls she chats with were discussing whether they would get married someday. M. writes, "Oh, I know I will. It is definitely my calling to be the wife of someone who serves God."

L. is a senior in high school and will soon graduate. His parents make him attend youth group, but he rarely says anything. He says he'd rather be out doing something. He is happy to participate in mission trips to help repair houses, and he recently worked with a community group to help put a new roof on the house of an elderly woman in his town. He is curious about how things work, and he thinks church people spend too much time talking about God instead of doing what matters. He wants to work with a local carpenter as an apprentice when he graduates, but he feels so different from the others in youth group that he just says, "I don't know," when asked to share his vocational goals. He wonders if everyone has to go to college to do God's work.

8

From God

CALL IS AN INVITATION. THE INVITATION COMES from God.

Let's visit Moses in the desert again to learn more about call. He is standing on a quiet hillside with one task to focus on— caring for the flock. The only sounds in the air are the bleating of the sheep and the call of birds. Perhaps a snake slithers through the rocks or grasshoppers leap from bush to bush, but otherwise everything is still. A burning bush would be pretty hard to miss.

❖ Call begins with an awareness of God.

How does Moses' experience compare to your daily life? Your generation is one of the busiest, most programmed, and overextended ever. It has been estimated that the modern teenager, whose days are filled with school, homework, extracurricular activities, Internet surfing, email, text messages, radio, television, books, newspapers, and magazines, receives more incoming information in a single month than a person in Bible times received throughout his or her *entire* life. Thanks to flip phones, MTV, BET, VH1, honking horns, woofers, advance-placement classes, soccer, math club, part-time jobs, and church, the life of an adolescent today is seldom still and rarely quiet. In the midst of a busy and noisy life, deliberate action is necessary to find time and space to become aware of God's presence.

For centuries spiritual people have practiced meditation to draw themselves away from the world and become open to God. Meditation can be as simple as a quiet walk, focusing on your breathing, praying in a quiet place, or listening to relaxing instrumental music. The meditation outlined below is based on the familiar children's song "Head, Shoulders, Knees, and Toes," so it is easy to remember. It can be done seated or lying down and takes only a few minutes. Why not try it out before you read on?

1. Sit or lie down in a comfortable spot and take two slow, deep breaths.

2. Continue breathing deeply and picture the golden light of God's love moving with relaxing warmth from the top of your head. . .slowly down to your shoulders. . .to your knees. . .and to the tips of your toes.

3. Take two slow breaths, and with each breath, imagine the light glowing stronger and flowing through the muscles of your neck, arms, tummy, legs, and back.

4. See the light spreading relaxing warmth to your eyes, ears, mouth, and nose as you continue to take slow, deep breaths.

5. Inhale slowly and think to yourself, "God loves me."

6. Continue with slow, deep breaths, mentally repeating, "I am loved," for as long you want to.[1]

The image of the burning bush in the Moses story tells us something about God. A bush that is ablaze but does not burn up is something completely outside of human understanding. The term *holy* comes from the Hebrew word for "other." To say that God is holy is to say that God is completely other than us, that the reality of God cannot be contained within human ideas. Awareness of God helps us to remember that we are not in charge. In God's presence we can be led in ways beyond the limits of human expectation and understanding, which is a handy thing when the future is unknown and uncertain.

During their encounter in the desert, God told Moses to take off his shoes because he stood on *holy* ground. Holy space is wherever people and God connect. It is in these connections, these holy spaces, that our awareness of God can move us toward our callings. Being aware of God is a beginning point, but it is not enough.

Sometimes people are aware of God and even have a relationship with God but still get off track. One of Christianity's earliest heroes was a man who headed down the wrong road but found out that even the wrong road could become holy space.

The Call of the Apostle Paul: Acts 7:58; 9:1-31

Like many Jews in his time, Saul had a Hebrew name and a Greek version of his name—Paul—that was used in the larger Roman society. Saul was a well-educated, devout leader in the Jewish community and also a Roman citizen, so he had quite a bit of power and freedom. The first Christians were Jewish, and they practiced their faith in Jesus in synagogues and house churches in Jerusalem and in the rural Jewish communities that Jesus had visited. Saul eventually became known as the apostle Paul, and he was responsible for spreading Christianity and establishing Gentile (non-Jewish) churches throughout the Roman Empire. But this apostle started out with a very different mission.

Saul had a relationship with God and, according to his Jewish faith, believed that blasphemy was a capital offense. He was convinced that the people of "the Way," as the first Christians were known, were committing blasphemy by preaching about Jesus. After Saul witnessed the stoning of Stephen, the first martyr of the Christian church, Saul was sure he had found his mission: He was to travel to the rural communities, arrest followers of Jesus, and bring them back to Jerusalem for trial. So with letters of authority from the high priest in his pocket, Saul headed off for the synagogues of Damascus.

Along the road, Saul was knocked flat by a bright light, and he heard a voice ask, "Saul, Saul, why do you persecute me?"

"Who are you, Lord?" Saul replied.

"I am Jesus who you are persecuting," was Jesus' response.

Paul, still blinded by the light, was led to the home of a follower of Jesus. There he sat alone, without eating or drinking. After three days, Ananias was sent by God to heal Saul's eyes. Ananias also baptized Saul, and the two men shared a meal. Saul stayed with the followers of Jesus for a few days, took some time to make sense of his new experience, then began his work as Paul, apostle of Jesus and preacher to the Gentiles.

❧　Discovering your call is grounded in a lifetime of getting to know God.

Saul had spent his life in relationship with God, but he found out there was so much more of God to know. Just like any relationship, a relationship with God takes time and effort. Have you ever had a conversation like the following?

"Hey, do you know Troy Brown?"

"Well, I know who he is, but I don't know him."

Knowing someone is more than knowing who he or she is. Knowing someone involves an ongoing relationship. Let's look at four ways people have been getting to know God since the beginning of time.

CELEBRATION. Have you ever heard someone say, "I feel so bad that I skipped church," or "Well, at least *I* go to church!" Somehow "worship" has become "going to church," which sounds kind of like doing a duty. If you've ever heard news reporters talk about the pope leading Mass, you may have noticed them say, "The pontiff *celebrated* mass." *Celebrated!* Worship is indeed celebration. When the Hebrew people worshiped, they sang, danced, told stories, and participated in rituals that reminded them of what God had done. The early Christians partied in joyful celebration, singing songs, telling the stories of Jesus, and eating meals together. True worship reminds us of God's love and draws us deeper into relationship with God.

PRAYER. With all the books on prayer and workshops for prayer, it could seem like prayer is complicated. But it isn't. Prayer is just conversation with God. There are no magic formulas. No things we *must* say. No things we *can't* say. Prayer can take place when we are seated in a church, walking in the woods, or lying on our beds. Prayer can be private or shared with others. It can be silent or expressed in words, music, or even movement. Prayer begins with knowing that God accepts us exactly as we are and finds joy in spending time with us. In prayer we can talk to God about anything. And in prayer we can listen to God. In the quiet, still moments of prayer, God can break through the many voices that fill our thoughts and speak to us with the voice that is heard in our hearts.

STUDY. The main written source for getting to know God is the Bible. The stories the Hebrew people told at their celebrations were eventually written down and became part of what we call the *Old Testament*. The stories of Jesus, along with stories and letters from the earliest churches, became our *New Testament*. Any call will be in keeping with who God is as revealed in the Bible. The Bible is a storybook that tells about God's dream for the world. The stories also tell about people, who sometimes were and sometimes were not in tune with God's dream. So getting to know God through the Bible means exploring, sometimes using tools, such as dictionaries and encyclopedias; asking questions; and learning from others. It also means using more than our minds. If we let the stories touch us and connect with our hopes, joys, fears, and disappointments, the Bible can draw us closer to God and can even change us.

ACTION. Think about a close friend. How did you get to be friends? Friends often get to know each other by doing things together. This is true in a relationship with God, too. It was when Saul was doing what he thought was the business of God that God redirected him. Then, when he came to understand that Jesus and God are one, he took action. He met with followers of Jesus. He was baptized. He traveled around and preached the gospel. Through these activities, Paul came to know God more and more. Actions that help us grow in relationship with God include participating in rituals, such as baptism and the Lord's Supper; serving in the church; and reaching out to help others.

For Reflection
❁ Call begins with an awareness of God.
❁ Discovering your call is grounded in a lifetime of getting to know God.

1. If you tried the "Head, Shoulders, Knees, and Toes Meditation," what was the experience like for you? Do you think it would be helpful for you to make meditation a regular part of your life? In what other ways might you find quiet and stillness?

2. Select one category below and respond to the questions related to it.

CELEBRATION
- Does worship seem like celebration to you?
- How could you change your approach to worship so that you find more celebration in it?
- How could worship in your church be changed to make it more celebratory?

PRAYER
- Do you have a favorite time, place, or way to pray?
- How might your prayers change if you believed you could say anything to God?
- How might your prayers change if you were expecting God to guide you during prayer?

STUDY
- If you were to think of the Bible as a collection of stories, would that change how you read it?
- Have you ever read a Bible story and thought, "Hey, I can relate to that"?
- What might help you feel more connected to the stories in the Bible?

ACTION
- Have you ever made discoveries about yourself while working on a project?
- Have you ever made discoveries about God while working on a project?
- If there were one thing you could do to help God's dream for the world come true, what would it be?

To You

CALL IS AN INVITATION THAT COMES FROM GOD. The invitation has your name on it.

Do you remember Sister Mary Robert from *Sister Act*, who helped us define *call* in chapter 1? After she spoke about her dream of having something special to do that only she could do, she became embarrassed and asked, "Is that bad?" It might seem conceited for people to say they are special and there's something important that only they can do, but it isn't! Knowing you are special and believing you have a unique calling mean you are simply accepting the truth about yourself and giving honor to God, who created you and calls you. If you still feel doubtful about being special and having a calling, though, you are in good company.

❖ God calls all people, regardless of past history, limitations, or situation.

Do you remember what Moses said after God called him—by name—and told him to go to Egypt to lead the slaves to freedom? Moses asked, "Who am I to do that?" Moses had some good reasons to doubt. He was a criminal on the run. When he was young, he lived luxuriously as Egyptian royalty at the expense of the people who suffered in slavery. His whole identity had been a lie. "Who am I to do this great thing?" was not a silly question for Moses. God's response to Moses' question, "Who am I?" was "You are mine. That's who you are." That's how God answers your doubts, too.

God's call is directed to you personally, just as you are. It is not a call for you when you fix all your mistakes, or when you are smarter or stronger, or when you get older. It is a call for the person you are right now. Some people might think that being young is a limitation. The prophet Jeremiah once thought that. In the Old Testament book that bears his name, Jeremiah tells the story of his call in poetry.

The Call of Jeremiah: Jeremiah 1:4-8

The word of the LORD came to me saying,
  "Before I formed you in the womb I knew you,
  and before you were born I consecrated you;
  I appointed you a prophet to the nations."
Then I said, "Ah, Lord GOD! Truly I do not know how to speak, for I am only a boy." But the LORD said to me,
  "Do not say, 'I am only a boy';
  for you shall go to all to whom I send you,
  and you shall speak whatever I command you.
  Do not be afraid of them,
  for I am with you to deliver you,
says the LORD."   (NRSV)

Jeremiah became one of the most important prophets of all time. More than twenty-five hundred years later, we are still learning from him. Some people might say that Jeremiah was called *in spite of* the fact that he was young, but it is quite likely that Jeremiah was called precisely *because* he was young. In chapter 6 we'll look more closely at the unique characteristics of the season of life called "adolescence" and explore how those characteristics make you *especially* suited to a certain type of calling, but for now, just know this: If you think that being young is a limitation for calling, think again!

Moses was born with a special identity that suited him to lead the slaves out of Egypt and across the desert twelve hundred years before the birth of Jesus. Jeremiah was born with a special identity that suited him to serve as a prophet to the people of Judah six hundred years after Moses. You were born with a special identity that suits you for a unique calling in the twenty-first century. You have abilities, passions, and perspectives that are crucial to your call. And you will continue to be gifted by God to fulfill your call throughout your life. So, before you can respond to God's call for your life, you must listen to who you are.

❧   Uncovering God's call requires getting to know your *self*.

This call to listen to yourself is not about self-centeredness or selfishness. It is about honoring yourself because God created you and God *needs* you to be you. We all are made in such a way that doing the things God created us to do fulfills us like nothing else—not money, not fame, not beauty, not intelligence—can. The greatest joy in life is to be our true selves, so finding your call means getting to know yourself. Getting to know yourself begins with listening to yourself, to others, and to God.

Listening to yourself involves listening to your:
- dreams to discover your passions
- experiences to find your strengths and weaknesses
- sadness to identify things you'd like to change
- joy to realize what makes you feel truly alive
- body to get in touch with truths you may be ignoring

Listening to others can help you:
- identify your gifts
- think about yourself in new ways
- explore new possibilities
- test out your ideas
- identify changes to make

Listening to God can give you:
- hope when you feel like giving up on yourself
- comfort when you feel like you'll never figure out who you really are
- motivation when you think you can't do anything right
- a place of acceptance, which is the best place to get to know yourself
- perfect love, which overpowers fear and can teach you to love yourself

The "For Reflection" section of this chapter has three parts that are designed to help you do some self-discovery. Before you begin, review each of the parts to decide which you want to focus on first.

For Reflection

❧ God calls all people, regardless of past history, limitations, or situation.

❧ Uncovering God's call requires getting to know yourself.

1. One important aspect of knowing who you are is to assess honestly how mature your faith is. Rate the statements below according to the following scale:

1 = Yep, that's me!
2 = Well, sort of.
3 = Nope, not me at all.

When you're done, make note of your strengths and identify some areas you'd like to grow in.

Faith Maturity Assessment[1]
- My faith is a source of satisfaction for me.
- My faith surprises me, challenges me, and helps me to grow.
- My faith brings me help from outside myself (God, other people, the Bible, prayer books, etc.).
- My faith puts me in touch with others' needs.
- My faith helps me to understand my experiences in life.
- My faith makes me open to new situations.
- My faith helps me to realize my potential as a person.
- The particular beliefs that make up my faith are different now than when I was a child.
- My faith allows me to live with unanswered questions.
- I am inclined to share my faith with others.

2. You have two primary sources for information about your strengths and skills: yourself and other people. Answer the questions below, then review your responses, paying close attention to any patterns.

Myself
- What holds your interest so much that you lose track of time?
- What are your strongest characteristics?
- What are your weaknesses?
- What do you feel happy about in the world?
- What do you feel angry or sad about in the world?
- Which subjects interest you most?
- If you could watch an educational film on any topic, what would that topic be?
- What was your proudest moment?

- What was your favorite game or toy when you were a child?
- What are the three most important things in your life?

Others
- If your friends were asked to describe you with three words, what would they say?
- If your siblings or cousins were asked to describe you with three words, what would they say?
- If the adults in your life (parents/guardians, grandparents, teachers, minister) were asked to describe you with three words, what would they say?
- Who do you think is right: your friends, siblings, parents, or grandparents? List those three qualities again.
- If no one is right, why do you think it is that people don't know the real you?
- Has anyone ever said, "Wow, you're good at that"? If so, what were you doing?
- How would you complete this sentence? Whenever _____ has to be done, they always call on me.

3. Think about a time when you were absolutely happy and felt completely alive. Spend some time thinking, writing, or drawing about that time. Use the following questions to guide your reflection.
- Where were you?
- Who were you with?
- What were you doing?
- What were you feeling?
- What made it such a good experience?
- What does this experience tell you about yourself?
- In what ways do past positive experiences influence your present and future? Why?

To Partnership

CALL IS AN INVITATION. THE INVITATION IS FROM God. It is addressed personally to you. The invitation is to partnership with God.

In our culture there seems to be two different understandings of Christianity. One understanding is that Christianity fits into the "religion section" of my life. The other understanding is that Christianity is a way of life.

Christianity as a Religion

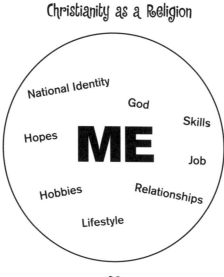

Christianity as a religion is when I call myself "Christian," yet I remain the center of my universe. I invite God into the circle of my life, alongside my career, hobbies, relationships, national identity, talents, education, possessions, and all the other ways I define myself. God is treated as *my* co-pilot. I turn to God to solve my problems. I expect God to map out a happy life for me. In return I go to church and try to follow rules that make me a good person. It's safe and self-focused. It's also boring and keeps things pretty much the way they are.

❉   Finding your call begins with the biggest "Yes!" of your life.

You may remember from chapter 2 that the first Christians were called "followers of the Way." For them Christianity was a way of life.

Christianity as a Way of Life

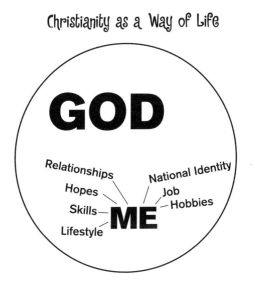

When I say yes to authentic Christianity, I step outside of the little circle of myself and bring everything—my relationships, my hopes, my fears, my career, my entire identity—into the context of God's dream for the world. I become one of God's co-pilots. My hopes, expectations, perspectives, and ways of relating are transformed, and I become a crucial player in God's work in the world. Saying yes is risky, God-centered, and exciting, and it has the potential to change both me and the world.

People say the big yes to God in a variety of ways. Some people have precise moments of being "saved," during which they become aware of God's claim on their lives and make a dramatic commitment to Christianity. Others gradually come to a commitment of faith. Both are equally authentic, and the differences usually reflect different personalities and backgrounds. If you have been raised in the church, you likely have had a variety of opportunities to say yes to God. Whatever way fits your personality and experiences is fine. What's crucial is making that decision, because your calling is revealed in the context of saying yes to God.

One of the most important and most well-known "yeses" in history came from the lips of a teenaged girl named Mary. You probably know about Mary from church Christmas pageants and holiday carols, but a closer look at her story can teach us some things about call.

The Call of Mary: Luke 1:26-38, 46-55

God sent Gabriel to Nazareth to deliver an invitation to Mary to have a son who would "be given the throne of King David," who would "reign forever," and "whose kingdom" would never end. After some initial concern because she wasn't married, Mary accepted God's call, saying, "Here am I, the servant of the Lord. Let it be with me according to your word."

Later when visiting with her relative Elizabeth, who was called to be the mother of John the Baptist, Mary celebrated in song:

With all my heart I praise the Lord,
and I am glad because of God my Savior.
He cares for me, his humble servant.
From now on, all people will say
God has blessed me. (Luke 1:46-48 TEV)

The Lord has used his powerful arm
to scatter those who are proud.
He drags strong rulers from their thrones,
and puts humble people in places of power.
God gives the hungry good things to eat,
and sends the rich away with nothing. (Luke 1:51-53 TEV)

Notice that Gabriel used the words *throne, reign,* and *king-dom* when talking about Jesus. Throughout the Bible, God's dream for the world is known as "the kingdom of God." This kingdom is not a place. Kingdom becomes real whenever people let God rule in their lives and whenever we work to make the world the way God intended it.

❧   Call is to partnership with God for the kingdom.

In Mary's song of praise, we catch a glimpse of what God's kingdom is like. Her song reflects the Old Testament understanding of God's kingdom and also anticipates the work of Jesus. The kingdom of God has been called an "upside-down kingdom" because it turns the ways of the world upside down. In place of self-interest, the kingdom creates community. In place of injustice, the kingdom calls for fairness. In place of oppression, the kingdom demands dignity and opportunity for all people. In the place of captivity, the kingdom seeks freedom. In place of exploitation, the kingdom requires care and respect for creation.

Establishing God's kingdom was a key part of Jesus' own calling. Jesus needed to explain his call to people around him, and he did that in a variety of ways. He did it when he welcomed people who were outcasts. He did it when he healed the sick, when he called people to be peacemakers, and especially when he died for us and rose again. And he did it in his hometown of Nazareth where people were wondering what in the world he was up to. They had seen him take his first steps. They had watched as he and their own children played together. They probably had patted him on the head and cleaned up his bruised knees. When Jesus visited the synagogue in his hometown, he made it clear that what he was up to in the world was bringing in the kingdom of God.

The Call of Jesus: Luke 4:16-20

He came to Nazareth where he had been reared. As he always did on the Sabbath, he went to the meeting place. When he stood up to read, he was handed the scroll of the prophet Isaiah. Unrolling the scroll, he found the place where it was written,

God's Spirit is on me;
he's chosen me to preach the Message
of good news to the poor,
Sent me to announce pardon to prisoners and
recovery of sight to the blind,
To set the burdened and battered free,
to announce "This is God's year to act!"

He rolled up the scroll, handed it back to the assistant, and sat down. Every eye in the place was on him, intent. The he started in, "You've just heard Scripture make history. It came true just now in this place." (MESSAGE)

Jesus began the work of making God's kingdom a reality, and he calls us to join him in continuing that work. The kingdom becomes real in each of our lives when we follow Jesus and say yes to God's dream, God's purposes, and God's plans. The kingdom becomes real in the world as we join in partnership with God and with others who have said yes and work to make the world a better place. Whenever God calls you, it is to *be someone special*. It is also to *do something special*. Your call is about both being and doing, just as it was for Moses, Jeremiah, and Mary.

For Reflection

❧ Finding your call begins with the biggest "Yes!" of your life.

❧ Call is to partnership with God for the kingdom.

1. Read the stories below to see how the church helped Kay and Larry say yes to partnership with God. In what ways have you said yes to God?

KAY: Growing up as a child in a warm, loving church, I felt special. The church gave me many opportunities to express my gifts in music, planning, and leading worship. An especially important person in my life was a deaconess (rather like a minister of education) who lived out her partnership with God in our church. Our pastors came and went, but Miss Louise stayed. She was always there to listen and to explain things about God I didn't understand. Once she told me that all of us young people in the church were like tiny seeds that God had planted in the earth. She said it was the work of the church to water those seeds so they could grow into healthy, beautiful plants. God provided the soil and the sunshine, but the church was to serve as God's partner by providing life-giving water and nourishment.

LARRY: My commitment to Jesus was different from Kay's. As a child, I listened to the sermons of my pastor and knew I wanted to be a Christian. But the time for making that commitment came for me at the conclusion of a vacation Bible school event at the age of nine. I knew I wanted to be a follower of Jesus, so I told my pastor I wanted to follow Jesus. I was baptized and tried to practice my new faith as best I could. When my family moved to another church, I was soon asked to teach younger boys in Sunday school. My partnership with God early on became one of using my gifts to teach others.

2. To learn more about God's kingdom, read one or two of the following passages.

Deuteronomy 15:1-11: the sabbatical year
1 Samuel 2:1-10: Hannah's prayer
Psalm 96: a psalm for worship
Micah 6:6-8: a message from the prophet Micah
Matthew 5:2-11 or Luke 6:20-31: the Beatitudes

3. Name some things in the world that you believe are contrary to God's kingdom.

4. In what ways can you imagine your gifts, skills, and interests serving God's kingdom?

In the Church and the World

CALL IS AN INVITATION FROM GOD THAT IS addressed to you. It is an invitation to partnership with God for the kingdom. It is also an invitation to partnership with others who say yes to God.

The Call of the First Disciples: Mark 1:16-20

As Jesus was walking along the shore of Lake Galilee, he saw Simon and his brother Andrew. They were fishermen and were casting their nets into the lake. Jesus said to them, "Come with me! I will teach you how to bring in people instead of fish." Right then the two brothers dropped their nets and went with him.

Jesus walked on and soon saw James and John, the sons of Zebedee. They were in a boat, mending their nets. At once Jesus asked them to come with him. They left their father in the boat with the hired workers and went with him. (CEV)

Jesus called his first four disciples on the same day, two at a time. The invitation to follow Jesus was also an invitation to join a group of followers. It is impossible to find and fulfill God's call without being connected to a community of faith. The words that are translated into English as "church" actually mean "an assembly or gathering of people."[1] The word *church* can refer to all Christians around the world or to local gatherings of people who celebrate, study, and serve together.

✿ Call is discovered and lived out in the local church.

It is helpful to think of churches as gatherings of people rather than as buildings. In the early years of Christianity, churches met in synagogues and in people's homes. Although many churches today meet in buildings that were built just for church, there are also gatherings in houses and other places. The New Testament uses many images to tell us what churches are about. The apostle Paul, whose call we talked about in chapter 2, was responsible for helping the churches he founded live as faithful communities. He did this by doing some visiting but mostly by writing letters.

Paul once received a letter from a church in the Greek city of Corinth telling him about heated arguments and cliques in the church. Paul wrote back, and his letter eventually became part of our New Testament. He described the church like this: "The body of Christ has many different parts, just as any other body does. Some of us are Jews, and others are Gentiles. Some of us are slaves, and others are free. But God's Spirit baptized each of us and made us part of the body of Christ" (1 Corinthians 12:12-13 CEV).

Paul didn't say the church is *like* a body. He said the church *is* the body of Christ! The call of churches is to be the very presence of Jesus in the world, to continue Jesus' ministry of God's kingdom. To do that, Paul insists, the church needs every person using his or her special gifts. "Together you are the body of

Christ. Each one of you is part of his body: First, God chose some people to be apostles and prophets and teachers for the church. But he also chose some to work miracles or heal the sick or help others or be leaders or speak different kinds of languages" (1 Corinthians 12:27-28 CEV). So the church is a community where you find your gifts and come to understand your call.

The church can help you discern your call by providing a place to experiment with different tasks and discover your strengths. Since it is sometimes difficult for people to recognize their own abilities, a major job of the church is to provide adults who can encourage you and help you identify and develop your talents. The Holy Spirit also gives people in the church particular abilities for the work of God's kingdom. These spiritual gifts come in two main types. Gifts such as hope and strength serve to build up the whole faith community. Abilities like teaching, prophecy, and service are given to individuals to meet special needs.

In addition to helping you discover your call by recognizing and nurturing your gifts and abilities, the church is also a place for "doing" your call. Some people make their living through church work, while others make their living outside the church. But *everyone* is called to serve in the church. Some churches are extremely large and have a number of paid staff people. In addition to pastors, large churches often have paid youth leaders, children's ministers, music ministers, educators, counselors, financial officers, building managers, secretaries, custodians, and parish nurses. Churches that are smaller now than they were years ago are finding new ways to have pastoral leadership. Since small churches have less money to work with and often cannot afford full-time pastors, more and more people are serving as bi-vocational pastors—that is, they have a job outside the church that provides their primary living, and they serve as pastor on a part-time basis.

How do you know if you have such a call? If you do, you will feel a strong inward tug that this is what you must do. You will also feel you have the abilities to do what is called for in such a role. You will have talked with other people who do what you think you are called to do. You will also need a strong will to keep on doing such a ministry, even when everything does not go well. Working for the church can bring disappointment— you must work with many kinds of people. They will not always agree with what you want to do. Making your living working for the church can be tough. But if this is your call, you will find joy in what you do. If there is not deep gladness, it is probably a sign you have misunderstood the call. You may not always be happy. But you will be blessed—full of the joy of the Spirit in your life.

If you think you may be called to professional church leadership, churches and denominations have ways of helping you think through that calling. The process usually begins with meeting with a committee whose job it is to help you discern and pursue your call. Moving forward in pursuing a call to professional church leadership involves specialized study, often with an internship in a local church; an intermediate form of recognition, such as being licensed to preach or ordained as an elder; evaluation by a designated group; and finally, recognition by a local church, a region, or a denomination in the form of ordination or commissioning that says, "We agree. This is your call."

There are also numerous ways to serve the church other than as a paid professional. You are probably familiar with people who lead the choir, teach Sunday school, and serve on church boards, but there are many other ways your gifts and skills can be put to work for the benefit of your faith community. Examples include lawyers and paralegals who guide the church in legal matters, carpenters and electricians who help with remodeling, seamstresses who make curtains and altar cloths, gardeners who care for the churchyard and provide flowers for the sanctuary, cooks who plan and prepare church dinners, and people with computer skills who prepare Web sites, bulletins, and newsletters. For the church to be all that God calls it to be, each member needs to take seriously his or her call to ministry. When the followers of Jesus fulfill their calling within the church, the church can fulfill its calling to the world.

After Jesus rose from the grave, he spent time with his followers to prepare them for the work they would do after he was gone. When it was time to say good-bye, Jesus made it clear that those who follow him are not to keep to themselves but are to go out into the world and continue his kingdom ministry.

The Call to Go Out to the World: Acts 1:6-11

When they were together for the last time they asked, "Master, are you going to restore the kingdom to Israel now? Is this the time?"

He told them, "You don't get to know the time. Timing is the Father's business. What you'll get is the Holy Spirit. And when the Holy Spirit comes on you, you will be able to be my witnesses in Jerusalem, all over Judea and Samaria, even to the ends of the world". (MESSAGE)

The most important work of the followers of Jesus is to reach out to the whole world, making God's kingdom a reality. Since God's kingdom is a kingdom of justice and wholeness, spreading the kingdom means meeting the world wherever injustice, sorrow, and sadness rule. We mentioned in chapter 1 that your call will satisfy you more than money, celebrity status, relationships, possessions, or anything else the world treasures. This is because your call draws on your gifts, your abilities, and especially on your passions to move the kingdom forward in the world.

❉ Your call's home address is the intersection of God's kingdom, your passions, and the world's pain.[2]

In chapters 2 and 3 we talked about how discerning your call requires getting to know God and listening to yourself. Finding your call also involves listening to the world to hear its cries for help. How do we listen to the world? Certainly newspapers, magazines, television stations, and Internet pop-ups report many of the problems of the world, but listening to all that negative information can be overwhelming without helping us to make a difference.

Christian denominations and ecumenical faith groups are a good source of information about the world's needs. They often also offer concrete suggestions for getting involved in solutions that reflect God's kingdom. Many denominations have Web sites and send out magazines or newsletters that are good resources. Some also have groups dedicated to researching and addressing particular problems, such as poverty, violence, and environmental destruction. As you pursue your call, it is a good idea to explore what your church, your denomination, and your local ecumenical groups (for example, a community council of churches) are doing to address needs in your town, your nation, and around the world.

For Reflection

❉ Call is discovered and lived out in the local church.
❉ Your call's home address is the intersection of God's kingdom, your passions, and the world's pain.

1. In what ways is your church the presence of Jesus in the world?

2. In what ways does your church family recognize and nurture your giftedness? How do you or could you use your skills and gifts to help your church be the presence of Jesus in the world?

3. When you fantasize about being a hero (and everyone does), what things do you accomplish?

4. What images have the power to make you cry? Here are some suggestions:

- a polluted stream
- a homeless person
- a serious illness
- The Trail of Tears
- tsunami victims
- a battered child
- a caged tiger

5. What images bring a smile to your face? Consider these:

- children learning to read
- an elderly man welcoming visitors
- a stray dog finding a home
- prayer in a hospital room
- a baptismal service
- feeding a hungry child
- a family talking things out
- enemies shaking hands

6. Read the story below. How does "A.'s" dream reflect call's "home address"?

A. enjoys science and the health channel on TV. She imagines herself working in an emergency room, helping people in pain. She might pursue a career as a physician or as a nurse. Either way, she is sure of her interest in crisis situations. At school she enrolled in a program in which adults come in and work with students to encourage them to do their best. When she's an adult, A. hopes to help young people by encouraging them in school and helping them find their way.

Now and Forever

CALL IS AN INVITATION TO PARTNERSHIP FOR GOD'S kingdom in this world. The invitation is from God to you. The invitation lasts a lifetime.

As we grow through life, we go through different times or seasons during which we have particular tasks to attend to and particular gifts to offer to our communities. The season of life called "adolescence" is very important personally because it is a time for laying the groundwork for healthy adulthood. It is also extremely important to the larger society because it is a time during which people are uniquely gifted to be a prophetic voice. Adolescents have always been major players in human history. For example, the American Revolution was won by people who were of high school age. What this means is that your call is not something you do in the future. It is something you have right now.

❧   Fulfilling your call now requires embracing adolescence.

Between the ages of thirteen and twenty, you are gaining new skills that are vital for understanding your call. Adults can give mixed signals about adolescence, sometimes pining away for the "carefree days of youth," sometimes grumbling about the nightmare of life with teenagers, and sometimes expressing sympathy—"I'd never want to go through those years again." Adolescence can be a tough time, but the very things that make it tough are also the things that make it a gifted time. No one knows better than you what these years are like; nevertheless, it may be helpful to look at the special characteristics of adolescence and see how those characteristics support your call. Adolescence is a time for:

DEFINING YOURSELF. If you are struggling with the question of who you are, you're doing what you're supposed to be doing. It's not easy, but it's necessary to struggle, explore, wonder, and dream now so that you can begin adulthood as the self God created you to be. Your work of exploring and finding your true identity can be a prophetic act, an activity that speaks louder than words. In seeking your identity, you can remind those around you that they need to engage in deliberate efforts to discover and become the persons God created them to be.

ASKING QUESTIONS. During your elementary years, you may have accepted a lot of things without questioning. Your early childhood, however, was probably filled with questioning. One of the great things about adolescence is that during the teen years, we reclaim some of the wonder of early childhood and begin again to ask questions—lots of them. Questioning helps you to determine what you truly believe and makes the faith *your* faith. Although it may be irritating to some of the adults in your life, your inquisitiveness can raise important questions through which people who have been in church for decades experience a reawakening of their own faith.

DREAMING BIG. Three gifts of adolescence are intensity, the ability to think about many possibilities, and an appreciation of others' experiences. So as an adolescent, you are uniquely gifted to see injustice, to believe passionately that things should change, and to imagine a better world. In his youth, Jeremiah began his career by reminding the people of God's dream for a just world: "If you truly act justly one with another, if you do not oppress the alien, the orphan, the widow, or shed innocent blood…then I [God] will dwell with you in this place" (Jeremiah 7:5-7, NRSV). People often say that adolescents are idealistic, complaining about unfairness in the world without recognizing practical realities. That may be true. But adults are often at the other extreme, so practical that they forget about God's dream for the world. As an adolescent, just like Jeremiah, you are uniquely gifted to remind others that making the world better is part of the calling of all Christians. Jeremiah has some more lessons to teach us about call.

The Lifelong Call of Jeremiah (Jeremiah 25 and 32)

Jeremiah lived a long life, and his call took on several forms over the years. In the early years, Jeremiah's main job was to warn the people and to call them to repent from injustice to create the kind of society God envisioned for them. Jeremiah met with huge disappointment while fulfilling that part of his call, as he told the people of Jerusalem: "For twenty-three years…the word of the LORD has come to me, and I have spoken persistently to you, but you have not listened" (Jeremiah 25:3, NRSV).

And because the people refused to change, their country was conquered town by town and the leaders and artisans were taken away to live in exile throughout the Babylonian Empire. Jeremiah's call then took on different forms. He wrote letters of encouragement to the people in exile, and he offered hope to the people left behind. Jeremiah's message of hope came through prophetic action as well as through his words. While Jerusalem was under siege, God told Jeremiah to buy a field. This was a ridiculous thing to do, because once Jerusalem was conquered, the land would be absolutely worthless. But Jeremiah did it anyway. He purchased a field from his cousin and presented the deed to the leaders of Jerusalem, saying, "For thus says the LORD of hosts, the God of Israel: Houses and fields and vineyards shall again be bought in this land" (Jeremiah 32:15, NRSV).

In the end Jerusalem fell and Jeremiah was forced to flee to Egypt, but his message of hope came true. Sixty years later the descendants of the exiles were allowed to return to the homeland and Jeremiah's words were preserved as the words of a true prophet.

�֍ Call unfolds as we walk through life.

One of the exciting things about call is that it unfolds throughout our lives. Each season of life has its own special tasks and gifts, and your call will unfold to make the most of your strengths throughout the seasons of your life. The world also changes and is in fact changing more rapidly and dramatically now than in the past. There's no way to fully anticipate what needs will be most pressing in the years ahead. Fortunately, your call will allow you to respond to a changing world.

All adults need to be able to provide for themselves, and one key area for living out call is livelihood. It is common these days for people to have four or more careers over their life span. And people often hold a number of jobs within a given career throughout their lives. This has been true in Kay's and Larry's experience.

KAY: I set out to be a missionary in Africa, but my choice to marry a man preparing for pastoral ministry helped me redirect my goals. I became a teacher. I've enjoyed teaching children, college students, and medical students. As a counselor, I also enjoy teaching families new ways of relating and approaching problems. Teaching and interacting with students has been my career, and I have fulfilled my calling within that career in several jobs in a variety of educational settings.

Along the way my career has taken unexpected turns. When our family was moving to a new city because of my husband's job, I expected to continue teaching and supervising student teachers as I'd been doing. I found a position and thought things were falling into place but then received a letter of rejection. I had to look for another type of work altogether. Yet every time a door closed, another opened, and in this case, the new direction provided a wonderful change in my life.

LARRY: As a high school student, I planned for my dream of pastoral ministry. Although I have been a pastor, I have also held other jobs within my career of professional church-related ministry. As a researcher and congregational consultant, I helped churches better serve their neighborhoods. I served as a school administrator, overseeing teaching and raising funds; and as a seminary teacher, I helped prepare future pastors. In all of these positions, I have lived out my call through the career of professional ministry.

I, too, have met with some surprises over the years. I was once convinced that God was calling me from teaching to a position helping urban churches. My wife and I talked and prayed, and we agreed the move was right for us. I felt secure in accepting the position, but in the end the leader of the organization did not approve my appointment. We accepted this as an indication that I was to stay in the work I was doing.

While most of us would prefer to sail easily through, life is complex and challenging. Sometimes it's the difficulties and disappointments that teach us about call. You've seen that in Jeremiah's story and also in our stories. Now consider an example from someone who is still early on in her journey toward call.

L. always enjoyed her English classes, especially the writing assignments. She wasn't sure if God was calling her to serve the kingdom as a teacher or a writer. L. decided to major in English and pursue teaching. During her junior year of college, she sat in on high school English classes. She was disappointed to discover that classroom teaching didn't suit her. She was still very interested in writing, but she knew that it could be difficult to make writing a career. L. works at a variety of jobs to support herself while she writes and submits manuscripts. The rejection slips have piled up, but that has only made her more determined to keep going. She believes this is her calling and that she has important things to say, so she pays close attention to critiques and advice and works hard to improve her writing. The effort is paying off. One of L.'s manuscripts has been accepted for publication.

Disappointment can become a stumbling block and interfere with moving forward in pursuing your calling. It can cause you to doubt your abilities and even to doubt that God has a unique calling for you. Disappointment can also be a guide. It can move you in a direction you hadn't anticipated. It can also challenge you to learn more about yourself and listen more closely for God's guidance. During times of disappointment, it is especially important to remember the mystery of God. God is beyond human understanding, but God isn't limited. Sometimes call unfolds in ways that are unexpected to us. But sometimes the unexpected is exactly what we need to better know God, ourselves, and our call. God's timing is wise, and we are perfected in our callings as we proceed with that understanding.

For Reflection

❊ Fulfilling your call now requires embracing adolescence.

❊ Call unfolds as we walk through life.

1. How is adolescence going for you? What parts do you enjoy? What parts make it difficult to bear? In what ways can you see being an adolescent as an important part of finding and fulfilling your call?

2. Think about a time you felt disappointed. What did it take to move past that feeling? Feelings give us information about ourselves. What could you learn from a disappointing experience?

3. Has there ever been a time when your life took an unexpected turn? Has the unexpected ever given you a nice surprise?

4. How can a relationship with God help you through the uncertainties of life?

5. Write a brief story, create a poem, or draw a picture of what you expect to be doing in ten years. Think about where you might be living, how you will be making a living, and how your dream will touch the world and further God's kingdom. After completing your story, poem, or picture, list the gifts and opportunities you have that will help you pursue this dream.

Book Title: _____

Your Comments: _____

_____

_____

Where did you hear about this book: _____

Reasons why you bought this book: (check all that apply)   □ Subject   □ Author   □ Attractive Cover

□ Recommendation   □ Gift   □ Other

If purchased: Bookseller _____ City _____ State _____

Please send me a Judson Press catalog. I am particularly interested in: (check all that apply)

□ African American   □ Baptist History/Beliefs   □ Children's Books

□ Christian Education   □ Church Supplies   □ Devotional/Prayer   □ Other

Yes, add my name to your mailing list!

Name (print) _____ Phone _____

Street _____

City _____ State _____ Zip _____ Email _____

Please send a Judson Press catalog to my friend:

Name (print) _____ Phone _____

Street _____

City _____ State _____ Zip _____ Email _____

JUDSON PRESS ■ P.O. Box 851 ■ Valley Forge, PA 19482-0851 ■ 1-800-458-3766 ■ Fax (610) 768-2107

Visit our website at www.judsonpress.com

BUSINESS REPLY MAIL

FIRST-CLASS MAIL   PERMIT NO. 6   VALLEY FORGE PA

POSTAGE WILL BE PAID BY ADDRESSEE

JUDSON PRESS
PO BOX 851
VALLEY FORGE PA 19482-9897

RSVP: Your Life

CALL IS AN INVITATION THAT COMES FROM GOD. The invitation is addressed to you personally and welcomes you to partnership with God for the kingdom—now and forever. Responding to God's invitation requires your whole life.

❊   Call affects all of your life choices.

God's call affects all aspects of who we are: lifestyle, career, leisure activities, and relationships.

One of the most important relationships you have in your life is the relationship with your self. If you are going to be able to fulfill Jesus' call to "love your neighbor as yourself" (Mark 12:31, NRSV), you must love yourself. We all have days when we feel good about ourselves and days when we don't like ourselves very much. Self-love isn't about how you feel. It is about what you do. It means taking actions that nurture your emotional, physical, and spiritual well-being.

As we mentioned earlier, your generation is one of the busiest ever. Many teenagers nowadays find it difficult to have "downtime", to get sufficient sleep, to eat right, and to get proper exercise. To fulfill your call, it is essential that you deliberately take care of yourself, even if it means doing things differently from others, to make sure you balance your active life with rest, worship, play, healthy eating, and regular exercise. Taking care of your self also means making wise choices about relationships. Whether friendships or romances, the types of associations you have can help or hinder your quest for your calling. It is important that you invest yourself in relationships that nurture you and avoid relationships in which you are mistreated or encouraged to participate in unhealthy behaviors.

The adolescent years are designed for maturing, and how well you accomplish the task of maturation depends in part on your key relationships. Maturity includes an ability to move beyond your own feelings to sense what life is like for others. It means having your world enlarged and putting your life into a larger perspective. It also means having the courage to deliberately develop your gifts by trying new things, even when you might fail and even if others may ridicule you. Friendships that help you expand your world and support your exploration of life are essential.

The story of Lydia provides an example of the importance of relationships in discovering and following your call.

The Call of Lydia: Acts 16:11-15, 40

Lydia was a first-century businesswoman who made her living selling exotic purple cloth. She lived in the city of Philippi, which was one of the stops for the apostle Paul and his companions Timothy and Silas on their tour to share the gospel. Lydia was a Gentile who had a relationship with the Jewish community. She was a non-Jew who believed in God and participated in Jewish worship.

Lydia also had relationships with a group of people who regularly gathered for prayer by a local river. One day Paul visited

Lydia's river gathering. Lydia was moved by his message, and she, along with the rest of her family, was baptized as a follower of Jesus. Afterward she insisted that the travelers come to her home and extend their visit. They were reluctant at first but were convinced when Lydia said, "If you have judged me to be faithful to the Lord, come and stay at my home" (Acts 16:15, NRSV). Lydia's home soon became a house-church, a place of gathering, study, and celebration for followers of Jesus.

Paul and Silas stayed with Lydia and continued to preach throughout Philippi. One day they were arrested, beaten, and put in jail. At night an earthquake shook the jail, and the two men were miraculously freed. A frightened city official insisted they leave town immediately, but instead the traveling companions went to Lydia's house to enjoy the company of Christians before moving on with their calling to spread the gospel.

Lydia's relationships were important in her call to serve God's kingdom. Her connection with the Jewish community made her able to accept the gospel when she heard it. Her family respected her and followed her lead in becoming a Christian. And she had like-minded friends who shared her faith and formed a church with her. Her calling was recognized and encouraged through these relationships.

Other aspects of Lydia's life were also key to her fulfilling her call to be a leader of a Christian church. Her work earned her respect in the community and provided her with a home that could be shared with others. The skills that made her a good businesswoman made her able to convince Paul and Timothy to stay at her home to continue their teaching in Philippi. Her leadership ability helped her oversee the faith community that met at her house.

Lydia was a merchant by trade. This may not seem like an obvious "Christian" career, but for Lydia it was. Some careers, such as pastoral ministry, international missions, and Christian counseling, may seem like obvious Christian vocations, while other jobs don't. The truth is that careers and jobs cannot actually be Christian or not Christian. It is people who are Christian or not, and work done in ways that reflect and promote God's kingdom is Christian work. While some jobs are obviously inappropriate for Christians because they are contrary to the values of the kingdom, many jobs can be part of call.

❋　Call affects what we do for a living and how we do it.

What we do for a living is important. Equally important, though, is *how* we do the work we do. For example, a pastor who dislikes his work and is resentful toward others probably has not found his calling. But a school bus driver who shows God's love to the children she transports and finds fulfillment in her life probably has discovered a job that fits her call. Defining "success" by our culture's standards is pretty easy—lots of money, a big house, nice vacations, and a fancy car. Success within the Christian faith is different—live faithfully; use your gifts, abilities, and resources for God's kingdom; have healthy relationships; and continue growing in your self-understanding and in your relationship with God. In short, success is discovering and fulfilling your call through your lifestyle, relationships, and livelihood.

Since making a living is such a big part of life and one key area in which you will live out your call, it is important to be purposeful in pursuit of your life's work. Key actions to take as you look to your future in general and your career in particular are to explore honestly, prepare responsibly, seek support deliberately, and dream big.

EXPLORE HONESTLY. One of the difficulties in determining which career we are called to is that jobs often look different from the outside than they do from the inside. Watching an episode of *Law and Order*, for example, might make you think you want to be a lawyer. However, the drama of closing arguments by television lawyers is quite different from the long hours of research and meetings that make up much of the practice of law in real life. It is important to look at careers honestly from the inside. You can do this by visiting with people who are engaged in particular work or by getting hands-on experience through volunteer work or an internship.

A second difficulty lies in identifying what about a given job actually appeals to you. Many people dream of being singers, actors, professional athletes, or politicians, when in fact what they really want is the wealth, fame, or sense of personal value they think such a career can give them. In our society, we overvalue and overpay certain professions, especially those in the entertainment and sports world. A good discovery technique is to carry out a career fantasy in your mind and then analyze what parts of the fantasy make you happy. Ask some pointed questions of yourself, such as: What do I hope this career will give me? Do I see myself making up for some lack in my life through this career? Would I still be interested in this career if it wouldn't make me rich, famous, heroic, or otherwise a "big deal"? Be gentle with yourself, but be completely honest. Making room for honest reflection in your planning opens the way for God to guide you.

PREPARE RESPONSIBLY. You can find information on preparing for careers through higher education or vocational training from your school guidance office. While a few generations ago a college degree nearly guaranteed finding a good job, that no longer holds true. Today many people with degrees are underemployed or even unemployed. While things will likely change in the future, this circumstance presents the opportunity to put formal education into proper perspective—that is, higher education and vocational training are valuable when they help you discern and follow the call God has for your life.

If you are blessed to live in a first-world nation, you probably have more education and career opportunities than are available in most places in the world. You may also be fortunate enough to come from a family that is able to help cover college costs. Jesus issued a clear directive about such blessing when he said, "From everyone to whom much has been given, much will be required" (Luke 12:48b, NRSV). There is a growing phenomenon of people treating college as a rite of passage and squandering those years as merely a time for personal adventure and exotic spring breaks. Education is a costly privilege that is not available to everyone. If you have the opportunity for formal training as a route to discover and pursue your call, then you need to fully appreciate that opportunity. That means doing some work ahead of time to find a program that will match your commitment, your skills, and your current understanding of your call. Setting aside time to do research can help relieve urgency that leads to premature choices, and it will also allow time for God to direct you.

SEEK SUPPORT INTENTIONALLY. With years of life experience to share, adults have much to offer you in your quest for call. Mentors are adults who help you explore and pursue your call. All people need mentors, as we can attest from our personal experiences.

> LARRY: I had an important mentor in a long-time friend who was also my supervisor in seminary. He was like a father to me in many ways. Once when I was considering a job change, he encouraged me to wait and explore other options. I listened, and soon my first teaching role developed.

If I had not listened to him, I would have missed many wonderful opportunities in my life.

KAY: In my training to be a therapist, I had a mentor who was a wise counselor and friend. He was older than I and had experience beyond my own. He provided a place for me to be trained as a therapist and told me about good books and resources. I learned more from him than I did from the books I read. I will never forget him.

Your church can be a good place to find mentors, and so can your school. The key is to seek out people who find fulfillment in their own lives and have your best interests at heart. True mentoring relationships are mutually respectful. Good mentors listen as much as they talk, offer advice when it is desired, and demonstrate trust in the people they mentor. As your interests become known, you will discover people who can support your dreams in a variety of ways.

DREAM BIG. God's dream for the world, known as the kingdom of God, is a huge dream. It is a world where people treat each other fairly, where no one goes to bed hungry, where creation is respected, and where all people celebrate the love of their Creator. God doesn't dream in little possibilities, and neither should God's people. God's call will propel you in directions you cannot imagine right now.

People often get trapped by the need to make a living and by prematurely taking on long-term responsibilities, such as marriage, parenthood, and home ownership, so that they hinder their ability to pursue big dreams. With all of its wonderful attributes, adolescence also has certain liabilities. One liability is impatience, a sense that if you don't do it soon, you won't ever do it. Dreaming big not only means imagining boundless possibilities; it also means long-range dreaming. All things come in proper time, so it is essential that you dedicate sufficient time to getting to know yourself and your God before you make life decisions that narrow your choices for years to come. When you graduate from high school, you will have lived approximately one-fifth of your life. You have four-fifths left and many wonderful things to do in partnership with the God who knows you, loves you, and calls you.

We wish it were possible to follow your story of God's call in your life for the future. But what is possible is for you to keep a record of your journey along the way. Why not write down a short dream you call "The Story of My Future!" If you don't like to write, make an audio or video recording. Then every year or so, pull it out and review how God's partnership has been fulfilled in your journey of faith. It is our hope you will be filled with gladness with what you discover.

For Reflection

❊ Call affects all of your life choices.

❊ Call affects what we do for a living and how we do it.

1. What relationships do you have that nurture you? Do you have any potential mentors?

2. Do you have any relationships that might interfere with the discovery of your call?

3. What careers have you daydreamed about? What do those dreams tell you about yourself?

4. Do you see any connections between God's dream and your dreams? What specific actions could you take this week to make those dreams come true?

Appendix for Leaders

WELCOME TO *CALL WAITING*. AS A LEADER OF youth, you have accepted a crucial calling. Your efforts are important, and the time and energy you will spend are tangible expressions of your faith and commitment. So in case no one else says it, we begin with a great big "Thank you."

Call Waiting has been designed with an eye toward maximum usefulness. It is written for individuals who want to explore God's call in personal study, making it a valuable resource for youth ministers, educational committees, and parents to share with youth and young adults. *Call Waiting* is also readily adaptable for small groups. This appendix provides seven weekly session outlines that can be adapted for a weekend retreat or week-long vacation Bible school. You need to be familiar with the flow of the book, and some sessions require advance preparation, so it will be helpful if you read through all the session outlines before leading a study.

One theme of *Call Waiting* is the lifelong task of getting to know yourself. A few minutes of reflection on the questions below will help you become aware of the strengths, weaknesses, expectations, and motivations you bring to this study. Such awareness will make you a more effective leader. So set aside all the "doing" for a moment, take a deep breath, "exhale" some of the demands that compete for your mental energy, and consider the following:

1. What was adolescence like for you?

2. Are there things you wish people had told you, offered to you, or allowed you to do during your adolescence and young adulthood?

3. As you envision working with youth, how do you see yourself interacting with them? What are your hopes? What would "success" look like to you?

4. How do you feel about "call" in your own life? Do you feel fulfilled in your day-to-day life? Where are your joys? Where are your frustrations? What are your resentments? Your fears? Your dreams?

5. In what ways do you see working with youth as part of your call?

6. Review the "Guiding Principles" on page 65 and spend some time reflecting on how to incorporate these principles into your leadership practices.

Guiding Principles

Youth ministry that is authentic and can transform lives is:

EMPOWERING, characterized by trust, hope, openness, freedom, respect, confidentiality, and respect.

NARRATIVE, seeking the intersection of the stories of God (as found in the Bible, in the life of the faith community, and in the experiences of faithful people), of self, and of the world as the place where Christian vocation is discovered.

CELEBRATORY, welcoming adolescence as a season of life gifted with an unspoiled and unfolding capacity for critical thinking that offers a needed prophetic voice and fresh eye to faith communities and their ministries.

CONTEXTUAL, nurturing connectedness to self, others, God, and creation and reclaiming the essential discipline of silence in the midst of the noisiness of the contemporary world, which holds most youth—and adults—hostage.

INCARNATIONAL, attending to the physical, emotional, and relational—as well as intellectual—needs of learners and welcoming the diverse modes of expression that make us human.

Using Call Waiting with Groups

Before you begin leading a study of call using *Call Waiting*, you will need to do the following:

1. Purchase string bags and make a gift bag for each participant with a Bible, a pen, and a copy of *Call Waiting*.

2. Review chapters and session outlines.

3. Print out each of the Key Points on a piece of heavy paper to post on the wall.

4. Outline the invitation from p. 4 on poster board, newsprint, or chalkboard.

5. Secure guests for session 7 to talk about how they live out their calls through their jobs. You will need a combination of church professionals and those who make their livings outside the church.

6. If you are going to use these sessions for VBS or a retreat, think about adding music, recreation, and additional group building activities. For weekend retreats, the following schedule is suggested:

Friday evening: arrival, dinner, sessions 1 and 2

Saturday morning: breakfast, sessions 3 and 4

Saturday afternoon and evening: lunch, session 5, recreation, dinner, session 6

Sunday morning: session 7

Session 1

PREPARE: Review chapter 1 and the session outline below. Post the invitation. Prepare a sample name card as described in "Gather." Gather materials: *gift bags; small index cards, various colors of fine point markers, hole punch, string, and scissors; newsprint and large marker or chalkboard and chalk; and key point posters "Call is something that all Christians share but that each of us has in a special way" and "Call is an invitation" and masking tape or pushpins.*

GATHER: As participants arrive, hand each a gift bag and an index card. Have them print out their first names vertically in the center of the card, in capital letters, then punch a hole and insert string to make a name tag. Once all have gathered, introduce yourself using your name card as a model. Direct an introduction activity as follows:

1. Use the letters of your name to create words or phrases that describe your skills, interests, or things you do that you are proud of. For example, using "SUE," I might do:

I like to **S**ki
I visit sh**U**t-ins
I **E**njoy math

2. Count off by twos to create two groups. Introduce yourselves using your name cards.

3. Count off by twos within the groups.

4. "Ones" switch groups and go through introductions again.

5. "Twos" of group one join with "ones" of group two and vice versa and do introductions once more.

Reconvene the large group and ask them to brainstorm words and phrases that come to mind when they hear the word *call.* Explain that you are going to explore call through Bible stories and there may be some surprises ahead.

EXPLORE: Either ask for a volunteer to read aloud "The Call of Moses" (p. 12–14) or review Moses' early years in Egypt and have a volunteer read aloud Exodus 3:1-12. Explore the story with discussion questions, such as:

- What was Moses' initial response to God's call?
- How do adults respond when you refuse to do what they ask?
- How did God respond? Did God insist, threaten, beg, or bargain?
- What important job did God want Moses to do?
- What promise did God make to reassure Moses?

Note that God told Moses he was the person for the job and promised to be with him but left the decision up to Moses. Read and post both key points for this session.

ENGAGE: Show the invitation outline and explain that in each upcoming session you will be focusing on one part of the invitation. Ask, "What ways do people respond to invitations?" and "Is it possible NOT to respond to an invitation?" Next, divide the participants into three groups and assign each group one of the stories to discuss from #7 from "For Reflection" in chapter 1 (p. 5–6). When they are done, invite the groups to share any advice or questions that arise.

DEPART: Explain that they will be given an assignment to do between sessions. Stress that the assignments are voluntary, but it will benefit them and the group as a whole if they prepare the assignments. Encourage them to respond by writing, drawing, discussing with a friend, or simply doing some reflective thinking—whatever works for them. The assignment for this session is #3 and #5 from "For Reflection" in chapter 1 (p. 5). Remind them to bring their string bags with them for each session. Gather in a circle and offer the following prayer or a brief one of your own: *Go from this time knowing that God loves you and has a special calling for you, and trust that God will be with you each moment of every day. Amen.*

Session 2

PREPARE: Review chapter 2 and the session outline below, paying special attention to the meditation you will be leading. Review four ways we get to know God (p. 13–14) and highlight portions you want to share with the group. Gather materials: *key point posters "Call begins with an awareness of God" and "Discovering your call is grounded in a lifetime of getting to know God" and masking tape or pushpins.*

GATHER: Hand out gift bags to any new arrivals. Review key points from session 1. Ask if any volunteers want to share the ways in which they can relate to Moses or ways they feel very different from Moses. Review the invitation and ask who issues the invitation. Read and post key point "Call begins with an awareness of God." Mention that one big difference between Moses and us is Moses' daily life—he lived close to nature, in a quiet world with time to think.

EXPLORE: Ask participants to think about Moses' encounter with God in the wilderness. Ask, "What strange things happened?" and "What did God say about the ground where Moses stood?" Invite suggestions for what *holy* means. It is likely that they will say things such as sacred, good, and pure. Explain that that is what *holy* has come to mean, but that the concept comes from the Hebrew word for "other" and indicates that God is completely outside of human experience and beyond human understanding. That's why getting to know God takes a lifetime. Read and post key point "Discovering your call is grounded in a lifetime of getting to know God."

Introduce the story of Paul by explaining that his story shows how even someone who thought he knew God well could discover that he was wrong. Ask for a volunteer to read aloud "The Call of the Apostle Paul" (p. 11–12). After reading, ask for comments or questions about the story.

ENGAGE: Review four main ways we get to know God (p. 13–14). Divide participants into four groups and assign each group one category from #2 from "For Reflection" in chapter 2 (p. 15). Reconvene and invite each group to share some of their responses.

DEPART: Remind participants that getting to know God takes time and effort. Note that both Moses and Saul encountered God in quiet, lonely spots (the wilderness and a barren road). Explain that perhaps the most challenging part of getting to know God in our age is the busy, noisy world we live in. Invite participants to share about their normal day: How much free time do they have? How often are they still? When is their world quiet? Explain that you are going to talk them through a meditation that they can use anytime to become quiet and listen for God. Explain that practicing this meditation at least once is their assignment, and point out that it can be found on page 10. Note that when the meditation is over, they will be free to leave whenever they feel ready and they should leave quietly. Invite them to get comfortable in their seats and close their eyes, then lead the following meditation:

1. Take two slow, deep breaths.

2. Continue breathing deeply and picture the golden light of God's love moving with relaxing warmth from the top of your head. . .slowly down to your shoulders. . .to your knees. . .and to the tips of your toes.

3. Take two slow breaths, and with each breath, imagine the light glowing stronger and flowing through the muscles of your neck, arms, tummy, legs, and back.

4. See the light spreading relaxing warmth to your eyes, ears, mouth, and nose as you continue to take slow, deep breaths.

5. Inhale slowly and think to yourself, "God loves me."

6. Continue with slow, deep breaths, mentally repeating, "God loves me," for as long you want to, and leave when you are ready.

Session 3

PREPARE: Review chapter 3 and the session outline below. Make a gift box by covering a small box in pretty paper and cutting a slit in the top for participants to insert index cards. Gather materials: *photocopies of the "Faith Maturity Assessment" (p. 22) for any who may have forgotten to bring their books; index cards and pens or pencils; cassette or CD of instrumental music and player; and key point posters "God calls all people, regardless of past history, limitations, or situation" and "Uncovering God's call requires getting to know yourself" and masking tape or pushpins.*

GATHER: As participants gather, ask for their honest responses to the meditation activity. Encourage them to keep at meditation to find a form that works best for them. It can be taking a walk in the woods, listening to instrumental music, or simply breathing deeply. Review the key points covered so far and the invitation. Note that today you are focusing on who the invitation is addressed to.

EXPLORE: Ask participants to think once again about Moses' encounter with God: What was Moses initial response? Why might Moses be resistant? We think of Moses as a hero, but who was he then (a criminal hiding out, a simple shepherd, and a man whose early life had been a lie)? Note that God's answer to Moses' question, "Who am I to do this?" was "You are *mine*, that's who you are!" Post and read key point "God calls all people, regardless of past history, limitations, or situation."

Offer an introduction to the story of Jeremiah's call, such as, "The prophet Jeremiah lived at a time of great change for God's people, when their little kingdom of Judah was caught between two warring superpowers. Jeremiah felt God's anger and sadness as the people stubbornly pursued their own ways. Jeremiah served as a prophet for more than 60 years, asking the people to change and offering words of comfort in hard times. This is the story of how it all began." Then read aloud Jeremiah 1:4-8 while the group follows along (p. 19 of *Call Waiting* or in their Bibles). Ask, "What hindrance did Jeremiah see to his call?"

ENGAGE: Remind participants that you've learned that finding your call requires getting to know God. Post and read key point, "Uncovering God's call requires getting to know your self." Have three volunteers read aloud the sections on "Listening to . . ." (p. 20–21).

Hand out two index cards and pens. Review the instructions (p. 21) and have participants privately complete the Faith Maturity Assessment. (Cheerfully provide copies to those who did not bring their books.) Assure them their responses will not be shared with others. When they have finished, ask them to write on one index card at least three strengths that they have and on the other card, two areas they would like to grow in. Be sure to participate in this activity yourself.

DEPART: Gather together in a circle around the gift box with the completed index cards. Explain that for their assignment, they have the choice of doing #2 or #3 of "For Reflection" in chapter 3. Encourage them to consider responding with poetry, artwork, or a story. Encourage them to take home the index card with their desired areas of growth and pray for God's help in growing in those areas. Point out the gift box and invite them to insert their "strengths cards" into the box to symbolize thanksgiving to God for those gifts. Start the music and insert your own strengths card to get things started. When all have added their cards, lead the group in laying hands on the box and offering a prayer of thanks to God for the gifted members of your group.

Session 4

PREPARE: Review chapter 4 and the session outline below. On poster paper or chalkboard, draw the circles representing Christianity as religion and as a way of life (p. 26, 27). Gather materials: *Bibles for any who forget to bring their gift bags; newsprint, markers, paper, and pencils; and key point posters "Finding your call begins with the biggest 'Yes!' of your life" and "Call is to partnership with God for the kingdom" and masking tape or pushpins.*

GATHER: Begin by reviewing the key points covered so far. Review the invitation and note that today you are focusing on the partnership we are called to with God. Explain that in our culture, there seem to be two understandings of Christianity. Review the circles, stressing authentic Christianity as a way of life. Post and read key point "Finding your call begins with the biggest 'Yes!' of your life."

EXPLORE: Ask volunteers to read aloud "The Call of Mary" (p. 28–30). Note the words *throne*, *reign*, and *kingdom*. Explain that God's dream for the world is known as the kingdom of God; the kingdom exists wherever people live as God wishes and whenever we work for a world that reflects God's will. Post and read key point "Call is to partnership with God for the kingdom." Explain that establishing God's kingdom was an important part of Jesus' own calling, as he explained to the people of his hometown of Nazareth. Read together Luke 4:16-20.

ENGAGE: Divide participants into three groups. Give each group one sheet of newsprint and a marker, and make paper and pencils available. Assign group one: Hannah's prayer (1 Samuel

2:1-9) and Mary's call (Luke 1:46-53). Assign group two: the sabbatical year (Deuteronomy 15:1-11), the message from Micah, (Micah 6:6-8) and the call of Jesus (Luke 4:16-20). Assign group three: Psalm 96 and the Beatitudes (Matthew 5:2-11 and Luke 6:21-31). Their task is to review the Scriptures and write on newsprint words and phrases that describe the kingdom. Next, ask each person to create a Cinquain poem about the kingdom following this pattern:

Line one: one-word title	Kingdom
Line two: two words or a two-word phrase	God reigns
Line three: three words or three-word phrase	When hungry eat
Line four: two words or a two-word phrase	Prisoners freed
Line five: title or synonym for the title	Kingdom

When they are done, invite them to post their poems and read them aloud. Keep their sheets of newsprint for use in session 7.
DEPART: Ask participants to do #3 and #4 of "For Reflection" in chapter 4 (p. 32) as their assignment. Invite them to turn to Luke 11:1-4. Explain that there are two different versions of the Lord's Prayer in the Bible: one in Luke and one in Matthew. Neither is exactly as it is usually recited in church, but all versions show how important God's kingdom is. Invite them to join with you in reading Luke 11:1-4 together as a closing prayer.

Session 5

PREPARE: Review chapter 5 and the session outline below. Prepare 6 large strips of poster board or other sturdy paper to represent roads and a square piece with "CALL" printed on it. Gather materials: *information on local, regional, national, and international ministries that help the poor and work for justice; colored markers; cassette or CD of instrumental music and* *player; and key point posters "Call is discovered and lived out in the local church" and "Your call's home address is the intersection of God's kingdom, your passions, and the world's pain" and masking tape or pushpins.*

GATHER: Once all have gathered, invite sharing on reflection questions: What do you see in the world that is contrary to God's kingdom? and How do you see your gifts relating to God's kingdom? Review key points so far and the invitation. Point out that today you are going to focus on the "where" of the invitation.

EXPLORE: Divide participants into three groups and assign texts: (1) Mark 1:16-20; (2) 1 Corinthians 12:12-13; and (3) 1 Corinthians 12:27-28. Reconvene and ask the groups the following questions:

■ GROUP ONE: How did Jesus call his disciples? Did he call them one at a time? Is the call to be a follower of Jesus also a call to be a part of a group? What do we call a group of disciples today?

■ GROUPS TWO AND THREE: What does Paul's letter to the church in Corinth say about the church? What does Paul call the church? Whose body is the church? What do you think that means? What does Paul say about different people in the body of Christ?

Post and read key point "Call is discovered and lived out in the local church." Summarize as follows:

■ As the body of Christ, the church is the presence of Jesus and the continuation of his ministry in the world.

■ The church needs all people with all their gifts and skills to fulfill this call.

■ Since the church is the presence of Jesus, our job is to take Jesus' ministry to the world.

Ask for a volunteer to read aloud "The Call to Go Out to the World" (p. 39–40). Post and read key point "Your call's home address is the intersection of God's kingdom, your passions, and the world's pain."

ENGAGE: Explain that you've discussed how call requires listening to God and listening to yourself, and now it is clear that call requires listening to the world. Ask for suggestions for ways to listen to the world. Set up a table with the materials you have gathered on local, regional, national, and international ministries that promote God's kingdom. Lay out two strips of poster board at each of three tables and ask for volunteers to label the strips "God's Kingdom," "My Passions," and "The World's Pain," so that each table has two strips with the same title. Invite the participants to spend time at each table, reviewing ministries and writing descriptive words or phrases on the "roads." When they are done, post the "CALL" square and arrange the road strips so the roads intersect at "CALL."

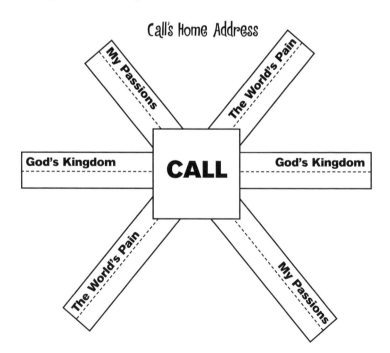

DEPART: Give #3, #4, and #5 from "For Reflection" in chapter 5 (p. 41) as the assignment. Explain that they will be given an opportunity to add to the "roads" next session and that the call/intersection poster they created will be presented in the church. Play instrumental music and close with a period of quiet meditation.

Session 6

PREPARE: Review chapter 6 and the session outline below. Make arrangements for your group to do a presentation on the topic of call using the call/intersection poster. This presentation could be at a meeting of a key church committee, as part of a youthled worship service, or at a special church gathering. Gather materials: *key point posters "Fulfilling your call now requires embracing adolescence" and "Call unfolds as we walk through life" and masking tape or pushpins.*

GATHER: As participants arrive, give them the opportunity to add to the call/intersection poster. Once all have gathered, review the key points so far and the invitation. Next, divide them into pairs to discuss how their church recognizes and uses their gifts; the ways they feel supported and welcomed in the church; and the ways they feel the church doesn't use their gifts. Encourage them to be honest, and stress the importance of confidentiality.

EXPLORE: Reconvene the group and review together the three special characteristics of adolescence (p. 45–46). Post and read key point "Fulfilling your call now requires embracing adolescence." Remind them that Jeremiah was called when he was very young and that it is quite likely he was called *because* he was young. Explain that they will be presenting the call/intersection poster to help remind the church of its calling to bring God's kingdom to the world. Spend some time preparing for this presentation, planning according to the arrangements you have made.

Explain that Jeremiah's call began when he was young and lasted for many years. Ask for a volunteer to read aloud "The Lifelong Call of Jeremiah" (p.46–47). Note that Jeremiah's call changed over the years and that he faced many disappointments. Post and read key point "Call unfolds as we walk through life."

ENGAGE: Lead a discussion on disappointment with questions such as: Can you remember a time when you were disappointed? What feelings did you have? What did it take to move past those feelings? Did you learn anything about yourself or the world through your disappointment? and How can a relationship with God help you through the disappointments of life?

DEPART: Gather participants around the call/intersection poster. Invite them to do #5 from "For Reflection" in chapter 5 (p. 50) as an assignment. Remind them of the details of your presentation and end with a prayer of blessing over the poster, asking that God might use it to help the church better fulfill its call.

Session 7

PREPARE: Review chapter 7, paying particular attention to key actions for pursuing life's work (p. 56–60), and review the session outline below. Secure guests to share stories of how they live out their call in their work. Be sure the guests know that you are making the point that both what we do and how we do it are related to call. Encourage them to prepare with a five-minute limit in mind. Also let them know that you will be talking about mentors and that they will participate in a closing prayer of support for the youth. Gather materials: *Christianity as religion and as a way of life circles from session 4; key point posters "Call affects all of your life choices" and "Call affects what we do for a living and how we do it" and masking tape or pushpins.*

GATHER: Once all participants have arrived, review the key points. Note the RSVP on the invitation and explain that this will be your focus. Show them the circle representing Christianity as a way of life. Post and read key point "Call affects all of your life choices." Ask them to identify some important choices made in life.

EXPLORE: Note the importance of relationships and how relationships in which we are respected help us fulfill our call. Read together "The Call of Lydia" (p. 54–56). Ask what key relationships are mentioned in Lydia's story and how they fit into her fulfilling her call. Mention that relationships were not the only part of Lydia's life that were important to her call. Ask participants to review Lydia's story and note ways her career and her skills served God's kingdom. Post and read key point "Call affects what we do for a living and how we do it."

ENGAGE: Give a brief summary of key actions to take in pursuing life's work: Explore honestly, prepare responsibly, seek support intentionally, and dream big. Introduce your guests and invite them to share about their jobs and call. Monitor presentations for time and allow time for questions.

DEPART: Invite the participants to share about their study with the guests. Encourage them to review the invitation, the key points, and the call/intersection poster. To close the study, gather the participants into a circle. Thank them for their participation and encourage them to continue journaling. Thank your guests and ask them to gather outside the circle, placing hands on the shoulders of the youth as a sign of their support for them. Offer a prayer, such as: *God, you call each of us to serve your kingdom. You have created each one of these young people with special skills and given each one a unique calling for your kingdom and the world. Bless them and help us to support them in their callings. Amen.*

Resources

Adrienne, Carol. *Find Your Purpose, Change Your Life: Getting to the Heart of Your Life's Mission.* New York: Quill, 2001.

Bolles, Richard N. *How to Find Your Mission in Life.* Berkeley, Calif.: Ten Speed Press, 1991.

Fowler, James W. *Becoming Adult, Becoming Christian: Adult Development and Christian Faith.* San Francisco: Jossey-Bass Publishers, 2000.

Hong, K. L. *Life Freaks Me Out: And Then I Deal with It: Reassuring Secrets from a Former Teenager.* Atlanta: Search Institute, 2005.

Levoy, Gregg. *Callings: Finding and Following an Authentic Life.* New York: Harmony, 1997.

Palmer, Parker J. *Let Your Life Speak: Listening for the Voice of Vocation.* San Francisco: Jossey-Bass, 2000.

Parks, Sharon Daloz. *Big Questions, Worthy Dreams: Mentoring Young Adults in Their Search for Meaning, Purpose, and Faith*. San Francisco: Jossey-Bass, 2000.

Ryken, Leland. *Redeeming the Time: A Christian Approach to Work and Leisure*. Grand Rapids: Baker, 1995.

Stevens, R. Paul. *The Other Six Days: Vocation, Work, and Ministry in Biblical Perspective*. Grand Rapids: Eerdmans, 1999.

White, David F. *Practicing Discernment with Youth: A Transformative Youth Ministry Approach*. Cleveland: Pilgrim Press, 2005.

Notes

Chapter 2
1. "Head, Shoulders, Knees and Toes Meditation," © 2001 Cassandra Williams, used and adapted by permission.

Chapter 3
1. Adapted from Stephen D. Jones, *Faith Shaping* (Valley Forge, Pa.: Judson Press, 1987), 104–5.

Chapter 5
1. "Church," in *The Learning Bible: Contemporary English Version* (New York: American Bible Society, 2000), 2174.

2. See Fredrick Buechner, "Vocation," in *Wishful Thinking: A Seeker's ABC*, rev. and expanded (San Francisco: HarperSanFrancisco, 1993), 118–19, for a fuller discussion of this idea.